User Guide to Samsung Galaxy S24 Ultra

Explore Every Feature of Your
Cutting-Edge Device

MASHA PAID

Table Of Content

Introduction

Welcome to the User Guide for the Samsung Galaxy S24 Ultra

Introducing the Samsung Galaxy S24 Ultra User Guide, your one-stop guide to maximising the capabilities of your state-of-the-art smartphone. Regardless of your level of experience with smartphones, this guide will help you get the most out of the Galaxy S24 Ultra by helping you navigate its features, functions, and capabilities.

Smartphones are essential in today's fast-paced technology environment because they keep us connected to the outside world and improve our digital experiences. With its cutting-edge features and cutting-edge technology, the Samsung Galaxy S24 Ultra leads the smartphone market.

Realising the Value of the User Manual
Studying the instruction manual thoroughly before using the Samsung Galaxy S24 Ultra is an essential first step. This extensive handbook is designed to provide you an understanding of the features, options, and capabilities of the device. This guide is your key to unlocking every element of your smartphone, whether it is taking amazing pictures with the new innovative camera system, maximising battery life, or exploring the newest connection choices.

Easily Navigating Your Smartphone
The Samsung Galaxy S24 Ultra is packed with features that may improve your everyday life, such its powerful CPU and dynamic display technology. This guide is organised to make

navigating through it easy for you. It offers detailed instructions, shortcuts, and advice on how to get the most out of your gadget.

You will learn about the camera technique, processing powerhouse, device architecture, and much more as you go through the chapters in this tutorial. Regardless of your interest in security features, customization possibilities, or resolving common difficulties, each part is designed to provide you with information and confidence.

Make the most out of your Samsung Galaxy S24 Ultra experience by reading through our user guide's abundance of information. Prepare to explore your smartphone's full potential as you set off on a journey of flawless connection, unmatched performance, and unmatched innovation.

We appreciate your choice in Samsung products, and now let's set out to maximise the potential of your Samsung Galaxy S24 Ultra!

Welcome to the Samsung Galaxy S24 Ultra User Guide

Congratulations on obtaining the cutting-edge Samsung Galaxy S24 Ultra smartphone. This premium model pushes the limits of innovation and technology. This user manual is a necessary travel companion that will help you fully use your sophisticated technology as you go on an exciting new adventure.

Handling the Digital Divide

Within the constantly changing smartphone market, the Samsung Galaxy S24 Ultra is a shining example of technical superiority. With its impressive camera system, tremendous performance capabilities, and wealth of advanced features, this phone is more than simply a phone—it's a doorway to endless possibilities.

Your Point of Entry into Innovation

The user manual serves as your road map as you set out on your adventure with the Galaxy S24 Ultra, assisting you in navigating the nuances of your new gadget. This book is designed to meet your requirements, whether you're a tech aficionado or a novice to smartphones. It offers thorough insights and directions.

Expectations

You will find comprehensive information regarding the device's design, features, processing power, camera proficiency, and much more inside the pages of this book. Every part has been designed to provide you with the necessary knowledge to fully use all of the features that the Galaxy S24 Ultra has to offer.

Handle Your Device Smoothly

Comprehending the significance of a user manual is essential for effectively exploring the extensive feature set that the Galaxy S24 Ultra provides at your disposal. This guide is your go-to reference for everything from initial device setup to investigating advanced camera settings and maximising battery life.

Accept the Opportunities

The Samsung Galaxy S24 Ultra is a gateway to productivity, creativity, and connectivity—it's more than simply a phone. Your key to maximising the functionality of your gadget and ensuring that you can easily incorporate it into your everyday life is this guide.

We appreciate you selecting Samsung, and we hope you enjoy this new chapter in smartphone history. Together, let's get off on this adventure where the Galaxy S24 Ultra connects you to a world of limitless possibilities and becomes an extension of your lifestyle.

Understanding the Importance of the User Guide

The Samsung Galaxy S24 Ultra User Guide is an indispensable resource in the rapidly evolving field of cutting-edge technology, offering customers insightful information and advice on how to get the most out of their smartphone experience. This user guide is essential reading for everyone interested in sophisticated smartphones, regardless of level of tech experience.

A Complete Source

The Samsung Galaxy S24 Ultra is a feature-rich handset with an abundance of functionalities. The user guide is an all-inclusive tool that you can use to navigate through the many features, settings, and innovations that this smartphone has to offer. Think of it as your digital buddy.

Exposing Secret Features

A smartphone's fundamental functions may be known to many users, but the Galaxy S24 Ultra opens up a world of secret capabilities, sophisticated settings, and cutting-edge tools. By revealing these hidden treasures and enabling users to investigate and incorporate them into their everyday lives, the user guide takes on the role of a lighthouse.

Debugging and Enhancement

When faced with difficulties or questions, the user handbook transforms into a troubleshooting guide, providing answers to frequently asked questions. This book provides customers with the necessary expertise to guarantee a smooth and hassle-free experience, covering everything from maximising battery efficiency to resolving connection issues.

Customised Instruction

Since each user is different, the user guide provides a customised learning experience in recognition of this variation. The guide is designed to accommodate individual requirements, regardless of your level of interest in learning about advanced capabilities, adjusting device settings, or becoming proficient with the camera system.

Filling up the Information Gap

The user guide connects users to the multitude of possibilities their Samsung Galaxy S24 Ultra possesses, acting as a bridge for those who are unfamiliar with the device. It serves as a teacher, guiding users through the initial setup, outlining important capabilities, and encouraging a better comprehension of the unique qualities that distinguish the Galaxy S24 Ultra apart from other smartphones.

Increasing User Self-Assurance

Gaining confidence from your equipment is facilitated by understanding it, and the user manual is an essential tool for doing so. With the help of the guide, users may become skilled users by taking charge of their device via step-by-step instructions, visual aids, and practical recommendations.

Essentially, the Samsung Galaxy S24 Ultra User Guide is more than just an instruction book—rather, it's a doorway to a more engaging smartphone environment. Think of this book as your reliable travel companion as you set out on your adventure with the Galaxy S24 Ultra—prepared to light your way to a world of opportunities and technical prowess.

Navigating Your Smartphone with Ease

The smooth and simple smartphone experience is the goal of the Samsung Galaxy S24 Ultra's design. To fully use your gadget, you must learn how to navigate around it. We'll go over some crucial hints and techniques in this part to make sure you can confidently and easily manage your Galaxy S24 Ultra.

Comprehending the Interface

The Galaxy S24 Ultra's user interface is a tasteful fusion of design and utility. The first step to being an expert on your smartphone is becoming familiar with the arrangement of the icons, menus, and navigation movements. You will be guided through each step of the user guide so that you can easily find and utilise the features you need.

Motion-Activated Navigation

With its array of gesture-based navigation options, the Galaxy S24 Ultra provides a seamless and intuitive way to use your smartphone. Discover how to use basic gestures to move between activities, access the home screen, and browse between applications. Your interactions with the smartphone seem more immediate and natural thanks to gesture navigation, which improves the user experience overall.

Personalising Your Home Display

You may improve usefulness and aesthetics by personalising your home screen, which is your digital canvas. Discover how to add widgets, change the background, and rearrange the app icons. You may design a customised, productive workplace that fits your use habits by customising your home screen.

Getting the Hang of Quick Settings

Keyboard shortcuts and important features are centralised in the fast settings panel. To have immediate control over features like Wi-Fi, Bluetooth, screen brightness, and more, learn how to access and modify fast settings. You may save time and effort by streamlining your regular interactions with the device by making effective use of the fast settings.

Multitasking Streamlined

The Galaxy S24 Ultra performs very well at multitasking. Learn how to use split-screen mode, move between open programs with ease, and take full advantage of the device's multitasking capabilities. The ability to multitask enhances productivity since it lets you switch between things without losing your pace.

Making Use of Edge Panels

With only a swipe, edge panels provide a handy way to access tools, applications, and shortcuts. Discover how to personalise the Galaxy S24 Ultra's edge panels by exploring the range of options available. Making effective use of edge panels enhances the ease of using your smartphone's navigation.

Voice Input and Integration with Bixby

Use voice commands to navigate your smartphone hands-free and take use of Samsung's virtual assistant, Bixby. Discover how to use your voice to do activities, set up instructions, and get information. Integration with Bixby improves usability and accessibility while offering a hands-free substitute for conventional navigation.

Using your Samsung Galaxy S24 Ultra is an efficient and informative adventure. The goal of this part of the user guide is to provide you with the information and abilities you need to easily operate your device. Making the most of your smartphone's sophisticated features and capabilities, you'll find yourself navigating its digital terrain with ease as you experiment with the tips and tricks provided here.

Chapter 1

Getting Started

The Samsung Galaxy S24 Ultra awaits you in a thrilling new world! We will walk you through the first stages of configuring your device in this introductory chapter so that you may start your trip with comfort and confidence. Getting started is essential to realising the full potential of your smartphone, whether you're upgrading to the newest Galaxy S series or opening your new one for the first time.

Contents and Unboxing

Give your Galaxy S24 Ultra some time to air before opening it to admire its svelte form and high-quality construction. Not only is there a smartphone in the box, but there are also other necessary accessories. Get acquainted with the contents, which usually consist of the gadget, a power adapter, a charging cord, and any other things unique to your area or carrier.

Putting the SIM Card in

It is essential that you install the SIM card that your cell provider provides before turning on your smartphone. Your SIM card serves as your entry point for mobile connection, enabling you to send and receive messages, make calls, and use mobile data. You will find detailed instructions in the user guide on where to find the SIM card tray, how to insert the SIM card properly, and how to secure it.

Turning On and First Configuration

It's time to turn on your Galaxy S24 Ultra after inserting the SIM card. While the smartphone is starting up, press and hold the power button until the Samsung logo appears. To begin the first setup procedure, adhere to the on-screen instructions. This involves logging in with your Google or Samsung account, choosing your language, and setting up a Wi-Fi network.

Facial and Fingerprint Recognition

You may improve your device's security by configuring biometric authentication techniques. Advanced face and fingerprint identification technologies are available on the Galaxy S24 Ultra. Your device will stay safe and secure while offering quick and easy access thanks to the user guide, which will walk you through the setup procedure.

Customising Your Device

Your taste and sense of style are reflected in your Galaxy S24 Ultra. Discover how to customise your cell phone by changing its theme, ringtone, and background. Personalising your gadget not only improves the user experience overall but also adds a personal touch.

Examining the Main Display

Your primary location for accessing features and applications is the home screen. Learn about the fundamentals of the home screen layout, including as shortcuts, widgets, and app icons. Comprehending the arrangement of the home screen is essential for effective navigation and multitasking.

Important Apps and Functionalities

Learn how to use the pre-installed applications and functions on your Galaxy S24 Ultra. The user guide will give insights into the operation of these essential apps, which range from the camera app to messaging and productivity tools. Learn how to use, navigate, and make the most of these applications for your everyday requirements.

You'll lay a strong foundation for your Samsung Galaxy S24 Ultra experience as you go through Chapter 1. In order to ensure that you can easily incorporate your new gadget into your digital routine, the user guide attempts to make the initial setup procedure as simple as possible. With the Galaxy S24 Ultra, be ready to discover all of the possibilities that lie ahead of you!

Unboxing Your Samsung Galaxy S24 Ultra

When the Samsung Galaxy S24 Ultra is revealed, there is excitement and expectation. The sensation of opening the box on your brand-new flagship smartphone sets the stage for the incredible features and functionalities that lie ahead of you. This section will walk you through the thrilling process of opening the package for your Samsung Galaxy S24 Ultra and provide you with information about what's inside.

Design and Aesthetics

Samsung recognizes the importance of aesthetics and that the first impression is sometimes the most enduring. The gorgeous design of the Galaxy S24 Ultra greets you as soon as you remove the outer cover and open the package. Give this gadget some time to appreciate its exquisite workmanship, svelte lines, and high-quality materials. It really is a piece of art.

Important Add-ons

A carefully chosen selection of accessories intended to enhance the features of the Galaxy S24 Ultra are included in the package. Among the prerequisites are:

- The Samsung S24 Ultra Mobile Phone

The centre of attention is your Samsung S24 Ultra. Feel the ideal harmony of innovation and elegance in your hands.

- A cable for charging

Take off the high-speed charging wire that comes with the charger. Quickly charge your smartphone by connecting it with ease.

- The Power Supply

Learn about the power adapter designed specifically to accommodate the Galaxy S24 Ultra's superior charging capabilities.

- Extra Items

You could also discover other things like paperwork, a SIM card extractor tool, and more, depending on your area and provider.

Insertion of SIM Card

Find the SIM card tray on your Galaxy S24 Ultra before proceeding with the setup. Insert the SIM card carefully to activate cellular access. To use mobile data, send messages, and place calls, you must complete this step.

Turning the Device On

Once the SIM card is firmly inserted, turn on your Galaxy S24 Ultra by pressing and holding the power button. Take in the vivid screen and the recognizable Samsung emblem, which mark the start of your trip with a smartphone.

Initial Thoughts

Spend some time examining the first set of on-screen instructions when the device powers up. Select your desired language, establish a Wi-Fi connection, and log in using your Samsung or Google account. The groundwork for a smooth and customised user experience is laid by these first actions.

Accepting the Ecosystem of the Galaxy

The Galaxy S24 Ultra is a doorway into the vast Samsung Galaxy ecosystem, not simply a smartphone. Discover how to build a harmonious and connected digital experience by exploring how your device combines with other Galaxy devices and services easily.

Unpacking the Samsung Galaxy S24 Ultra is the beginning of an incredible technical adventure rather than just the act of opening a box. Samsung makes sure that opening your Galaxy S24 Ultra is an unforgettable and engaging experience by paying close attention to detail and prioritising customer satisfaction. After taking your gadget out of the box, be ready to explore all of its features and potential!

Inserting SIM Card and Memory Card

Improving storage space and guaranteeing faultless connection are crucial measures in making the most out of your Samsung Galaxy S24 Ultra. We'll walk you through the process of putting a memory card and a SIM card into your smartphone in this section. Enabling cellular capabilities and adding more storage for your applications, movies, and images requires following these instructions.

- SIM and Memory Card Tray Location

Start by figuring out which memory card and SIM tray are on your Galaxy S24 Ultra. This tray, which is often found on the side of the gadget, may hold a microSD memory card in addition to a SIM card.

- SIM Ejector Tool Use

Samsung usually includes a SIM ejector tool in the packaging with the accessories and paperwork. This little tool is essential to accessing the SIM and memory card tray, so get it now.

- Removing the Tray

The little pinhole next to the SIM tray is where you should place the SIM ejector tool. Press gently until the tray comes out. The SIM card and memory card slots are visible when the tray is carefully pulled out.

- SIM Card Placement

Put your SIM card in the tray's designated slot. Make that the card slides into the designated slot firmly and that the metal contacts line up. For you to be able to utilise mobile data, send messages, and make calls, you must have a SIM card.

- Memory Card Insertion (Optional)

Now is the perfect time to insert your microSD memory card if you want to increase the amount of storage you have available. Make that the memory card fits tightly in the correct slot on the tray. Your Galaxy S24 Ultra can hold additional images, movies, and data if you insert a memory card.

- Putting the Tray Back in Place

Gently slide the tray back into the device after inserting the SIM card and memory card. Verify that it inserts easily and flush with the device's frame.

- Turning On Your Samsung S24 Ultra

Switch on your Galaxy S24 Ultra after making sure the memory card and SIM card are firmly inserted. You'll soon be able to access more storage and improved connection once the device powers up, allowing you to fully use the capabilities of your smartphone.

  You may ensure a fully functional and connected device by following these instructions to install the SIM card and memory card into your Samsung Galaxy S24 Ultra. These basic procedures guarantee that your Galaxy S24 Ultra is prepared to fulfil your communication and storage demands, whether you're making calls, taking pictures, or downloading applications.

Powering On and Setting Up Your Device

Best of luck with your brand-new Samsung Galaxy S24 Ultra! It's time to turn on your device and configure it for best usage now that you've unboxed it and put the SIM and memory cards in. We'll walk you through all the necessary steps in this part to power on your device, set up the basic settings, and make sure the setup goes well.

Turning On Your Samsung S24 Ultra

Once the Samsung logo shows up on the screen, press and hold the power button on the side or rear of your smartphone. Your Galaxy S24 Ultra will start up when you release the button. As the gadget turns on, please wait patiently.

Selection of Language and Region

Your Galaxy S24 Ultra will ask you to choose your favourite language and location when it first turns on. To choose the choices that best fit your location and preferences, tap on the corresponding ones.

Finding a Mobile Network or Wi-Fi

Please connect your device to a Wi-Fi network before continuing with the setup. You have the option to utilise mobile data if you don't currently have access to Wi-Fi. Maintaining the most recent version of your device and finishing the setup need a reliable internet connection.

Sign in using your Google account (optional)
To use individualised services like Gmail, the Google Play Store, and contact syncing, log in with your Google account. In this stage, you may establish a Google account if you don't already have one.

Sign-in to your Samsung account (optional)
You may backup your device's data and access only Samsung services by logging in with your Samsung account. During the setup procedure, you have the option to log in or establish a new Samsung account.

Setup of Biometric and Security
By configuring biometric capabilities on your Galaxy S24 Ultra, such fingerprint or face recognition, you may improve security. To register your biometric information and provide your device an additional degree of security, adhere to the on-screen instructions.

Check and Agree to the Terms and Conditions
Examine the terms and conditions that were provided to you throughout the setup procedure. Before continuing, make sure you read the conditions and agree to them. To use all of the features and services on your smartphone, you must complete this step.

Customising Your Gadget
Personalise your Galaxy S24 Ultra with wallpaper, themes, and further customization choices. Customise your smartphone to reflect your own style by choosing a look that fits with it.

Finalising the Configuration

After completing the basic setup procedures, your Galaxy S24 Ultra will be operational. Examine the settings, app drawer, and home screen to get acquainted with the device's UI.

You can make sure that your Samsung Galaxy S24 Ultra is seamless and customised by following these instructions for turning it on and setting it up. Whether you are an experienced smartphone user or a novice, these basic setup procedures provide the groundwork for you to fully use the capabilities of your Galaxy S24 Ultra.

Unlocking Your Smartphone: Security Features

When it comes to your Samsung Galaxy S24 Ultra, security is crucial. To secure your personal information, this section will walk you through the several security options on your smartphone. Examine your smartphone's unlocking choices and choose the one that best fits your demands in terms of security and personal taste.

1. Identification by Fingerprint

Using fingerprint recognition to unlock your Galaxy S24 Ultra is among the safest and fastest methods available. To configure and use this biometric capability, follow these steps:

- Open "Settings" on your mobile device.
- Make the choice "Biometrics and Security."
- Select "Fingerprint Recognition."
- To register your fingerprint, adhere to the on-screen instructions.

- After registering, you may quickly and easily unlock your smartphone with only a touch of your fingerprint.

2. Identification by Face

Unlock your smartphone using face recognition and enjoy the ease of the future. To configure face recognition:

- Select "Settings."
- Make the choice "Biometrics and Security."
- Select "Face Recognition."
- To record your face's features, adhere to the instructions.
- When it's finished, your Galaxy S24 Ultra will open with a simple look by recognizing your face.

3. PIN, Pattern, or Password

For those who choose for conventional techniques, establishing a password, PIN, or pattern offers a dependable means of safeguarding your gadget:

- Make use of "Settings."
- Select "Biometrics and Security."
- Click on "Screen Lock Type."
- To generate your security code, choose "Password," "PIN," or "Pattern," and then follow the steps.

4. Cognitive Scanning

With Intelligent Scan, you may combine the capabilities of iris and face recognition. This function determines the safest unlocking technique depending on your surroundings dynamically:

- Proceed to "Settings."
- Make the choice "Biometrics and Security."
- Select "Intelligent Scan."
- To configure Intelligent Scan, adhere to the on-screen directions.

5. Safe Storage

Use the Secure Folder feature to improve your privacy by giving your data and applications a secure location. To configure a secure folder,

- Click the "Settings" application.
- Select "Biometrics and Security."
- Choose "Secure Folder" and adhere to the setup guidelines.
- To see the protected material within the folder, use your favourite unlocking technique.

6. Remote Unlocking - Locate My Phone

Samsung's Find My Mobile feature lets you unlock your cell phone remotely in case you forget how to unlock it. Make sure this functionality is activated for you:

- Click "Settings."
- Open "Biometrics and Security."
- Choose "Find My Mobile" and allow unlocking by remote.

You may pick an unlocking technique or combination that best suits your needs and keeps your Samsung Galaxy S24 Ultra safe by investigating these security features. Your smartphone has cutting-edge security features to protect your digital life, whether it's the ease of face unlock, the quickness of fingerprint identification, or the dependability of a password.

Chapter 2

Device Layout and Functions

To fully use your Samsung Galaxy S24 Ultra, you must be familiar with its design and features. This chapter offers a thorough examination of the functions and physical attributes of your gadget, enabling you to use it with ease and take full advantage of its state-of-the-art capabilities.

1. Front Panel
Your Galaxy S24 Ultra's front panel has both a beautiful display and necessary sensors. Examine the following components:

- Show:
The large, bright screen offers a captivating visual experience, which makes it perfect for work, gaming, and entertainment.

- Primary Camera:
The front camera, housed inside the display, lets you take sharp selfies and make video calls.

- Light Ambient and Proximity Sensors:
These sensors improve the usefulness of the smartphone by sensing when the device is near your face during calls and changing the screen brightness.

2. Rear Panel

The primary camera configuration and other functions are located on the back of the device:

- Primary Cameras:

With its many lenses, the sophisticated rear camera system captures a wide range of situations with remarkable clarity and detail.

- Snap:

The flash makes low-light shooting better, guaranteeing detailed and well-lit images under difficult lighting circumstances.

- Microphone:

When taking pictures or using voice-activated functions, a specialised microphone captures sound.

3. Ports and Side Buttons

Look around the edges of your Galaxy S24 Ultra to find the different connectors and buttons:

- Bixby/Power Button:

This button, which is located on the right side, turns the smartphone on or off and brings up the Bixby virtual assistant.

- Buttons for Volume:

The volume buttons, which regulate audio levels during calls, media playing, and other audio-related activities, are located next to the Power/Bixby button.

- SIM Card Holder:

Your SIM card is kept in the SIM card tray, which is on the top or sides, for network access.

- Port USB-C:

Usually located at the bottom, the USB-C connector makes it easier to connect external peripherals, transmit data, and charge devices.

4. Biometric Sensors

Advanced biometric sensors on your Galaxy S24 Ultra provide safe and practical device access:

- Fingerprint Scanner In-Display:

The fingerprint scanner is built into the touchscreen and enables safe and rapid unlocking.

- Iris scanning and facial recognition:

For increased convenience, these front-facing sensors provide an additional biometric unlocking option.

5. Extra Functionalities

Examine other features and sensors that enhance your device's overall functionality:

- Presenters:

Immersion audio experiences are provided by high-quality speakers for calls and multimedia content.

- Wireless Charging Coils:

When compatible, wireless charging coils provide simple cordless charging.

Comprehending the arrangement and capabilities of every element enables you to optimise the performance of your Samsung Galaxy S24 Ultra. You will get a thorough grasp of the device's physical design and how to make the most of its capabilities as you explore the features covered in this chapter.

Exploring the Physical Features of the Galaxy S24 Ultra

With its exquisite appearance and plenty of cutting-edge physical features, the Samsung Galaxy S24 Ultra will redefine the quality of your smartphone experience. This section offers a thorough examination of the device's physical characteristics along with insights into its design and features.

Amazing Front Panel and Display

The Galaxy S24 Ultra's brilliant display, a technical wonder that enthrals consumers with its clarity and brightness, is its primary feature. In addition to housing the large screen, the front panel has necessary sensors that enhance the device's overall performance.

Display

With vivid colours, fine details, and an engrossing viewing experience, the Galaxy S24 Ultra's display is a visual marvel. Every interaction is improved by the display's excellent quality and responsiveness, whether you're browsing material, playing games, or watching films.

Front Camera

The front camera, which is intended to take sharp selfies and enable video chats, is tucked away within the display. The thoughtful arrangement guarantees a smooth transition between design and utility.

Proximity and Ambient Light Sensors

The gadget has proximity and ambient light sensors to improve user experience. These sensors maintain peak performance throughout calls by dynamically adjusting screen brightness depending on surrounding circumstances.

Attractive Back Panel

When the Galaxy S24 Ultra is turned, a complex back panel including the main camera configuration and other features becomes visible.

Main Cameras

The device's main attraction is its back camera system, which has many lenses with different functions. The cameras provide very good quality and versatile images, even in ultra-wide pictures and close-ups.

Flash

An essential part of low-light photography, the flash works in tandem with the cameras. Even in difficult lighting situations, the flash guarantees well-lit and detailed photos.

Microphone

The back microphone, when positioned carefully, improves audio capture for voice-activated tasks like video recording, adding to the immersive multimedia experience.

Simple Side Ports and Buttons

Examining the sides of the Galaxy S24 Ultra, one finds a well-considered layout of ports and buttons that highlights practicality and ease of use.

Power/Bixby Button

Located on the right side, this button has two purposes: it may be used to turn the smartphone on or off and to activate Bixby, Samsung's virtual assistant.

Volume Buttons

The volume buttons provide tactile control over audio levels during media playing, calls, and other audio-related functions. They are located next to the power button.

SIM Card Tray

The SIM card tray holds the SIM card and allows network access. It is positioned strategically on top or on the sides.

USB-C Port

Located at the bottom, this adaptable interface may be used to connect external peripherals, transmit data, and charge the device.

Innovative Biometric Measurements
The advanced biometric sensors of the Galaxy S24 Ultra combine ease and security.

In-Display Fingerprint Scanner:
The fingerprint scanner, which is neatly integrated into the display, offers a safe and practical way to unlock the smartphone.

Iris scanning and facial recognition
These sensors, which are on the front panel, provide consumers with customizable security and alternate biometric unlocking choices.

Comprehensive Sound and Extra Features
The Galaxy S24 Ultra's physical ensemble is completed with features that improve overall usefulness and audio quality.

Speakers
The gadget has excellent speakers that provide deep, engrossing audio for calls and multimedia entertainment.

Wireless Charging Coils
Wireless charging coils provide a simple and cordless charging experience for customers with suitable accessories.

Examining the Galaxy S24 Ultra's external components reveals a tasteful fusion of state-of-the-art technology and careful design. Every element has been painstakingly designed to provide them a gadget that is beautiful to look at and works well. You will find a device that offers a premium smartphone experience and fits in smoothly with your everyday life when you interact with these physical features.

Understanding Button Functions and Ports

The Samsung Galaxy S24 Ultra's well-thought-out buttons and connectors make navigating the device simple and easy. This section offers a thorough explanation of how to use the buttons and ports on the device to do different tasks.

1. Bixby/Power Button

The device's Power/Bixby button, which is situated on the right side, performs a variety of purposes that improve accessibility and user control.

- Power On/Off

To turn the gadget on or off, press and hold the Power/Bixby button.

- Activation of Bixby

Samsung's virtual assistant, Bixby, may be quickly pressed to start voice commands and information access.

2. Buttons for Volume

The Volume buttons, which are next to the Power/Bixby button, provide tactile control over audio levels for several purposes.

- Level Up/Down

To adjust the level of audio during conversations, media playing, and other audio-related operations, press the upper or lower portion of the Volume button.

3. Tray for SIM Cards

Network communication is facilitated via the SIM Card Tray, which is positioned strategically on the top or sides of the device.

- Inserting SIM Card

Gently remove the SIM Card Tray using the SIM ejector tool that is supplied.
- After positioning it in the appropriate slot, place the SIM card on the tray.
- Gently slide the tray back into the apparatus.

4. Port USB-C

The USB-C connector, which is located at the bottom of the device, is a multipurpose interface.

- Charging

Attach the included USB-C cable to the port in order to charge the gadget.

- Data transmit

To transmit data between the device and a computer or other compatible devices, use the USB-C connector.

- Connecting Accessories

Use the proper adapters to connect accessories, such as external drives or headphones.

5. Fingerprint Scanner on Display

The In-Display Fingerprint Scanner, which is perfectly integrated into the display, offers a quick and safe way to unlock the smartphone.

- Unlocking the smartphone

To unlock the smartphone, place your registered fingerprint on the specified region of the display.

6. Iris scanning and facial recognition

These biometric sensors, which are situated on the front panel, provide additional ways to unlock the smartphone.

- Face Recognition

By glancing at the front camera, register your face characteristics to unlock the smartphone.

- Iris Scanner

Align your eyes with the sensor to unlock the smartphone using the iris scanner.

Users may maximise the potential of their Samsung Galaxy S24 Ultra by becoming familiar with the button functions and connectors. Every feature, whether it's controlling SIM cards, turning on the smartphone, modifying audio settings, or using biometric unlocking techniques, makes the user experience smooth and easy to use. You'll see how the Galaxy S24 Ultra enhances your regular interactions with ease and adaptability as you explore these features.

S-Pen Integration Unleashing Creative Potential

One unique feature that makes the Samsung Galaxy S24 Ultra stand out is the S-Pen's integration. The S-Pen, which is well-known for its accuracy and adaptability, completely changes and elevates the smartphone experience. This section delves into the creative possibilities that the S-Pen on the Galaxy S24 Ultra unlocks.

1. Easy Matching
The S-Pen and Galaxy S24 Ultra link with ease, establishing a snappy and quick connection. Users may take use of a variety of features meant to boost creativity and productivity once linked.

2. Accuracy and Sensitivity
The S-Pen replicates the feel of a conventional pen and paper for writing and sketching thanks to its improved tip and pressure sensitivity. By varying the pressure used, users may precisely annotate and add detailed features to designs by changing the line thickness.

3. Command in the Air
When you activate the Air Command menu, a wealth of functions become available, all you have to do is hover over or click the S-Pen button.

- Create Notes

Quickly scribble notes or drawings on the screen; they will be stored for future use.

- Screen Write

Directly annotate screenshots by adding drawings or remarks that are specific to you.

- Smart Select

Choose and take screenshots, pictures, or videos from the screen.

4. Convert While Travelling

With its quick translation capability, the S-Pen removes the obstacle of language boundaries. The S-Pen is a fantastic tool for language aficionados and tourists alike. All you have to do is hover the pen over foreign text to get real-time translations.

5. PenUp

PenUp provides a specialised area for budding artists and doodlers to exhibit their work. Create digital works of art, show them out to the PenUp community, and delve into the motivating realm of creative expression.

6. Optimising Productivity with S-Pen

The S-Pen improves daily productivity in addition to artistic endeavours.

Notes may be quickly taken on the screen, even while the device is locked, and stored for later use using the Screen Off Memo feature.

- Intelligent Magnification

Make use of the S-Pen to enlarge text on the screen for a more detailed examination, improving legibility.

7. Adjustable S-Pen Parameters

Customise each user's S-Pen experience by adjusting the device settings. Make the S-Pen an extension of your imaginative and efficient personality by adjusting the sensitivity, personalising Air Command shortcuts, and exploring a variety of other settings.

The Samsung Galaxy S24 Ultra's incorporation of the S-Pen goes beyond traditional smartphone use, making it an effective instrument for expression, productivity, and creativity. The S-Pen unlocks a world of possibilities at your fingers and improves the user experience overall, whether you're a digital artist, an avid note-taker, or someone who appreciates accuracy in interactions. See all the many ways that the S-Pen may enhance your creative activities and change the way you interact with the Galaxy S24 Ultra.

Chapter 3

Display and Visual Experience

The Samsung Galaxy S24 Ultra has an advanced display that raises the bar for visual quality. This chapter explores the intricacies of the gadget's display technology, offering consumers a thorough how-to manual for maximising the visual experience.

1. AMOLED XE Dynamic Display

The Dynamic AMOLED XE display is the brains behind the Galaxy S24 Ultra's impressive visual capabilities. With its ability to produce vivid colours, deep blacks, and unmatched clarity, this display technology creates an atmosphere that makes for an engaging visual experience. Discover the captivating universe of entertainment with vivid colours and striking contrast.

2. Adjustable Rate of Return:

The gadget has an adjustable refresh rate that modifies itself intelligently according to the material being seen. The display smoothly switches between refresh rates for both fast gaming and smooth article scrolling, maximising battery life and performance.

3. Resolution in WQHD+

Every detail on the screen is enhanced by the WQHD+ resolution, which produces clear and sharp images. Whether you're reading text, looking at pictures, or watching high-definition movies, the Galaxy S24 Ultra's display promises an eye-candy experience with breathtaking clarity.

4. Support for HDR10+

Thanks to HDR10+ support, enjoy entertainment with gorgeous contrast and lifelike colours. Experience content like the creators intended with the Galaxy S24 Ultra, whether you're streaming your favourite programs or taking and viewing HDR-enabled images.

5. Immersion from Edge to Edge

With as little bezel as possible, the edge-to-edge design of the display maximises screen real estate for an incredibly immersive experience. With its large screen, you can enjoy multimedia material, multitask while gaming, and every moment is preserved in cinematic quality.

6. Constantly-On Display

Take use of the Always-On Display function to be informed quickly. Even while the smartphone is in sleep mode, you may customise the display to show important information like the time, date, and notifications.

7. Blue Light Filter

Put your eyes' comfort first with the Blue Light Filter function, which lessens eye strain from extended screen time. Turn this feature on to enjoy more screen time without sacrificing eye comfort.

8. Mode with One Hand
With One-Handed Mode, navigating a huge screen becomes simple. One-handed access to information, applications, and settings easily improves the user experience overall.

9. Customization of Display Settings
Adjust the display settings to meet personal tastes. Modify the text size, brightness, and colour balance to create a customised visual environment that suits your particular viewing preferences.

10. Optimizations for Gaming
The Galaxy S24 Ultra's display has been optimised to provide gamers with better gaming experiences. Take pleasure in snappy touch interactions, lag-free visuals, and a seamless gaming experience.

With unmatched brightness, the Samsung Galaxy S24 Ultra's display brings every detail to life, serving as more than simply a window into your digital world. Explore the many features and settings that make the Galaxy S24 Ultra display a genuine standout in the world of smartphone technology, and dive into the depth of colour, clarity, and innovation. The Galaxy S24 Ultra display raises the bar for immersive and engrossing viewing experiences, whether you're a multimedia fan, content producer, or someone who appreciates visual perfection.

The Dynamic Display Technology: A Visual Delight

In the ever-evolving landscape of smartphone technology, the Samsung Galaxy S24 Ultra stands out as a beacon of innovation, and at the forefront of its captivating features is the Dynamic Display Technology. This section delves into the visual delight offered by the Galaxy S24 Ultra's dynamic display, providing users with insights into the cutting-edge technology that makes every interaction a feast for the eyes.

1. Dynamic AMOLED XE: Redefining Brilliance
The Galaxy S24 Ultra boasts a state-of-the-art Dynamic AMOLED XE display, setting new standards for visual excellence. With an emphasis on vibrant colours, deep blacks, and high contrast ratios, this advanced display technology ensures that every image, video, and graphical element is presented with stunning clarity and precision. Prepare to be immersed in a world where colours come to life, and details leap off the screen.

2. Adaptive Refresh Rate: Smoothing the Visual Journey
One of the hallmarks of the Galaxy S24 Ultra's display technology is its Adaptive Refresh Rate. This intelligent feature dynamically adjusts the refresh rate based on the content being viewed, ensuring seamless transitions and optimal performance. Whether you're scrolling through social media, watching videos, or engaged in high-speed gaming, the display adapts to deliver a smooth and responsive visual experience.

3. WQHD+ Resolution

The WQHD+ resolution takes clarity to the next level, presenting images with remarkable precision and detail. Whether you're exploring high-resolution photos, reading text, or streaming videos, the Galaxy S24 Ultra's display ensures that every pixel contributes to a visually stunning and immersive experience. Witness content in cinematic quality right at your fingertips.

4. HDR10+ Support

Elevate your visual journey with HDR10+ support, a feature that brings content to life with true-to-life colours and enhanced contrast. Whether you're capturing photos with HDR-enabled settings or streaming HDR content, the Galaxy S24 Ultra ensures that you experience the full spectrum of colours and details as intended by content creators.

5. Edge-to-Edge Immersion

The Galaxy S24 Ultra's display is not just a window; it's a canvas that extends from edge to edge, minimising bezels to maximise your viewing pleasure. Immerse yourself in content without distraction, whether you're gaming, watching videos, or multitasking. The expansive display creates a truly cinematic experience that captivates and engages.

6. Always-On Display

Stay informed without unlocking your device with the Always-On Display feature. Customise it to show essential information such as the time, date, and notifications, even when the device is in standby mode. Efficiency meets elegance as the Galaxy S24 Ultra keeps you connected with just a glance.

7. Blue Light Filter: Prioritising Eye Comfort
Caring for your eyes is paramount, and the Galaxy S24 Ultra's Blue Light Filter is designed with that in mind. Reduce eye strain during extended screen time by activating this feature, striking a balance between captivating visuals and visual comfort.

8. One-Handed Mode: Navigating with Ease
The large screen of the Galaxy S24 Ultra is designed for immersive experiences, but navigating it with one hand is made effortless with One-Handed Mode. Access your favourite apps, settings, and content with ease, providing a user-friendly touch to the visual grandeur of the device.

9. Display Settings Customization: Your Visual Preferences
Tailor the display settings according to your unique preferences. Adjust brightness, colour balance, and font size to create a personalised visual environment that aligns with your individual taste. The Galaxy S24 Ultra puts the power of customization at your fingertips, ensuring that your visual experience is precisely how you want it to be.

10. Gaming Optimizations: Elevating the Gaming Realm
For avid gamers, the Galaxy S24 Ultra's display comes with dedicated optimizations to enhance the gaming experience. Enjoy smooth graphics, minimal lag, and responsive touch interactions as the display immerses you in the thrilling world

of mobile gaming. The combination of visual excellence and gaming prowess makes the Galaxy S24 Ultra a true companion for entertainment enthusiasts.

- Elevating Visual Standards

The Dynamic Display Technology of the Galaxy S24 Ultra is more than just a specification; it's a testament to Samsung's commitment to setting new visual standards in the smartphone arena. From the brilliance of the Dynamic AMOLED XE display to the thoughtful features like Adaptive Refresh Rate and HDR10+ support, every aspect is meticulously designed to provide users with a visual delight that transcends expectations. As you embark on your journey with the Galaxy S24 Ultra, prepare to witness a world where visuals are not just seen but experienced in their full splendour. Welcome to the future of smartphone displays—welcome to the Galaxy S24 Ultra.

Adjusting Display Settings for Optimal Viewing

Users of the Samsung Galaxy S24 Ultra may customise their visual experience to suit their own tastes by navigating the vast array of display options. This section offers a thorough tutorial on how to modify the display settings for the best viewing experience, making sure that the amazing features of the device's display are fully used.

1. Brightness

To get the best viewing experience possible, set brightness first. You may find the brightness settings under the Display section in Settings or in the quick settings menu. To get the ideal balance between sharp images and battery life, move the brightness bar. Finding the proper brightness offers clarity without straining your eyes, whether you're in a well-lit area or watching material in a less lit one.

2. Let Your Phone Learn with Adaptive Brightness

For an intelligent function that adapts to your preferences, turn on Adaptive Brightness. This feature automatically changes brightness according to your use habits and environment. Adaptive Brightness adjusts the display for different lighting situations over time according to your preferences, resulting in a constantly pleasant viewing experience.

3. Screen Timeout

To combine power saving with convenience, choose the screen timeout duration. Navigate to the Display section under Settings to access this adjustment. By customising the screen timeout length to your specific use patterns, you can make sure that the display turns on when you need it and shuts off when not in use.

4. Night Mode: Convenient Low-Light Viewing

By lowering the amount of blue light that the display emits, Night Mode—also referred to as Blue Light Filter—improves eye comfort when used at night. Locate this option in the Display settings, then set it up to turn on automatically at certain times. Night Mode reduces blue light, which lessens eye strain and improves the comfort of reading or browsing at night.

5. Font Style and Size

Users may alter the look of text on-screen by adjusting the Font and Style options. To make the text easier to read and in line with your choices for style, make adjustments to the font size and style. The Galaxy S24 Ultra gives you the option to customise the device's appearance, so you may choose a bolder, bigger font for easier reading or a more sophisticated look.

6. Customised, Natural, or Vivid Screen Mode

With its several screen settings, the Galaxy S24 Ultra can accommodate a range of visual tastes. Vivid, Natural, or personalise the display to your preference are your options. While Natural offers a realistic and well-balanced portrayal, Customised lets users adjust colour settings to create a unique visual style. Vivid intensifies colours for a more vivid experience.

7. Dark Mode: Elegant and Energy-Sparing

By changing the visual interface's colour to a darker tone, Dark Mode helps OLED screens last longer on batteries and lessens eye strain in low light. You may set Dark Mode to operate just during certain hours and turn it on or off according to your preferences. This function optimises power consumption and gives the UI a fashionable touch.

8. Inconspicuous Alerts: Edge Lighting

Discover how to get aesthetically pleasing, unobtrusive alerts by using the Edge Lighting function. Tailor the colour and style of the edge lighting to your own preferences. This function ensures that you keep updated without interfering with your viewing experience by elegantly enhancing incoming alerts.

9. Customised Scaling for Screen Zoom and Font Adjustments

Modify the Screen Zoom settings to fine-tune the scale of on-screen material. To make sure that text is shown at a size that is suitable for your eyes, you may also personalise font changes. By accommodating users' preferences for bigger or smaller components on the screen, these capabilities provide an additional degree of customization.

10. Finding the Correct Balance Between Display Quality and Resolution

Look at possibilities for changing the resolution and quality of the display under the Display settings. Despite the Galaxy S24 Ultra's high-resolution capabilities, users may choose settings that strike a compromise between battery economy and visual quality. Discover the ideal balance that fits your needs and habits on how you use your devices.

- Customising Your Visual Tour

Tailoring the Galaxy S24 Ultra's display settings is more than simply customisation; it's about designing a visual experience that fits your own tastes. Through brightness adjustments, the activation of intelligent functions, and customization of the visual elements of the display, users may fully use the impressive display technology of the device. Take charge of how you see the world via the lens of your smartphone as you set off on your visual adventure with the Galaxy S24 Ultra.

Night Mode and Blue Light Filter: Enhancing User Comfort

Two crucial features—Night Mode and Blue Light Filter—are introduced by the Samsung Galaxy S24 Ultra in an effort to provide a fluid and pleasant viewing experience. These features not only improve the comfort of the user while using the device at night, but they also lessen eye strain and promote general eye health.

1. Night Mode: Quiet Darkness for Exploration at Night

The purpose of Night Mode, sometimes called Dark Mode, is to change the device's interface's colour scheme to a darker one when there is less light. By turning on Night Mode, you may dim the display's overall brightness and change the colour scheme to a darker range of tones. This reduces eye strain while using the device in the dark and gives the interface a fashionable touch.

- How to Turn on Night Mode
- Open the Settings menu.
- Choose Display.
- Toggle Night Mode on by finding it.

To further personalise Night Mode and guarantee a smooth transition between day and night viewing, users may schedule Night Mode's activation during certain hours. In addition to making for a more soothing visual experience, the muted colour palette saves battery life, particularly on smartphones with OLED screens.

2. Blue Light Filter: Enhancing Ocular Well-being

One function that is specifically designed to support eye health during extended use—especially in the hours before bed—is the Blue Light Filter. Digital displays generate blue light, which may disrupt sleep cycles and lead to eye discomfort. The Blue Light Filter on the Galaxy S24 Ultra lessens the amount of blue light that the display emits, allaying this worry.

- Steps to Turn on the Blue Light Filter:
- Select Settings.
- Choose Display.
- Find the Blue Light Filter and turn it on.

The Blue Light Filter's schedule and strength may be further adjusted by users to suit their unique needs. Users may have more pleasant viewing sessions and more peaceful sleep by limiting their exposure to blue light, particularly at night.

Blue Light Filter and Night Mode Benefits
- Reduced Eye Strain

The Blue Light Filter and Night Mode both help to lessen eye strain, especially after prolonged use.
- Improved Sleep Quality

Reducing exposure to blue light before bed may improve sleep quality and encourage a more wholesome sleep-wake cycle.
- Longer Battery Life

By using Night Mode, which has a dimmer colour scheme, you may help OLED displays use less power and have longer battery lives.

Chapter 4

Camera Mastery

The Samsung Galaxy S24 Ultra is proof that the camera has evolved into a crucial component in the world of smartphone innovation. This chapter explores the camera system's finer points, revealing the features that elevate the Galaxy S24 Ultra to the status of a photographic powerhouse.

1. Penta-Lens Configuration

The groundbreaking Penta-Lens design, a five-lens combination that pushes the limits of mobile photography, is at the core of the Galaxy S24 Ultra's camera system. Together, these painstakingly made lenses serve a particular function and enable photographers to produce photos with unmatched clarity and detail.

Penta-Lens Configuration Overview

- 108MP Wide Lens

Great for taking detailed photos and large-scale landscapes.

- The Periscope Telephoto Lens

provides superior optical zoom for far-off objects.

- Ultra-Wide Lens

Ideal for obtaining a wider viewpoint and taking panoramic photographs.

- Macro Lens

Stunning close-ups reveal the beauty of minute details.

- DepthVision Sensor

Accurately sensing depth enhances portrait photography.

2. Pro Mode

Pro Mode on the Galaxy S24 Ultra turns novice photographers into experienced ones, giving users more control. With the use of Pro Mode, users may manually adjust a variety of camera settings, including exposure, focus, and white balance. Every photo becomes a masterpiece because of the new creative possibilities this degree of control brings.

Main Characteristics of Pro Mode

- Manual Focus

To have exact control over the focal plane, adjust the focus points.

- Exposure Control

Adjust exposure levels to provide the best possible contrast and brightness.

- White Balance Adjustment

To create the ambiance you want, adjust the colour temperature.

3. Intelligent Photography AI-Powered Improvements

Artificial intelligence (AI) is included into cameras to improve their capabilities, which makes photography more rewarding and intuitive. The AI-powered scene recognition feature of the Galaxy S24 Ultra's camera system makes sure that every picture is automatically adjusted for the subject, lighting, and composition.

- Features Enhanced by AI
- Scene Recognition

Recognizes scenarios automatically and modifies parameters for best outcomes.

- Smart Composition

Provides on-screen recommendations to assist users in composing aesthetically pleasing images.

4. Cinematic Captures

The Galaxy S24 Ultra is an excellent camera for capturing dynamic scenes with a cinematic touch, going beyond static photography. With the ability to shoot films in up to 8K resolution, users may produce videos of high quality straight from their smartphones.

Features for Video Recording

- 8K Recording

For unparalleled clarity, record videos in breathtaking 8K quality.

- Super Steady Mode Provide smooth, polished films by stabilising footage.
- Director's Perspective While filming, fluidly transition between several viewpoints to create engaging narrative.

Revolutionary Camera System Overview

Samsung continues to push the frontiers of smartphone photography with the launch of the Galaxy S24 Ultra, a handset that breaks beyond traditional limits thanks to its innovative camera technology. This part offers a comprehensive overview, elucidating the nuances of the camera setup that takes the craft of moment capture to new heights.

1. The 108MP Wide Lens: The Ultimate in Pixel Power

The amazing 108MP wide lens of the Galaxy S24 Ultra is the foundation of its exceptional photographic capabilities. Your device's high-resolution sensor serves as its eyes, enabling you to take stunningly detailed and clear pictures of situations. The 108MP wide lens makes sure that every pixel in the picture, whether it's a close-up or panoramic panorama, conveys a narrative.

2. Periscope Telephoto Lens: Accuracy in Every Pixel

The technical miracle that gives the Galaxy S24 Ultra strong optical zoom capabilities is the Periscope Telephoto Lens. With this lens, you may put an end to distance restrictions as it perfectly clarifies distant things into focus. Zoom in to make the details pop, whether it's a far-off mountain top or a sight of animals.

3. Broad Horizons: Ultra-Wide Viewing Angle

The Galaxy S24 Ultra's Ultra-Wide Lens opens the door to limitless creativity. Using a wider angle, capture the majesty of expansive vistas, group portraits, or architectural wonders.

With the help of this lens, you may abandon traditional framing and see and capture more in a single picture.

4. Macro Marvels: Revealing the World of the Microscope

The Galaxy S24 Ultra's Macro Lens is a surprise for anyone who values beauty in the little things. Explore the world of microbes and capture minute details and frequently overlooked beauties. The Macro Lens highlights hidden beauty, such as the exquisite patterns on a butterfly's wing or the fine veins of a leaf.

5. Creating Artistic Portraits with DepthVision Sensor

The Galaxy S24 Ultra's DepthVision Sensor is a creative as well as a technological innovation. It allows you to take professional-looking photographs by measuring depth accurately. Attain an exquisite bokeh effect that softly blurs the backdrop, emphasising your subject.

6. Video Excellence: Symphony in Motion

The Galaxy S24 Ultra is a cinematic storyteller that you can hold in your hands, not merely a camera for taking still images. The device's 8K resolution recording capacity turns every movie into an artistic work of art. Relive everything with unmatched clarity and detail, from routine daily events to grand experiences.

Capturing Moments: Photography Tips and Tricks

Embark on an infinite creative journey with the Samsung Galaxy S24 Ultra. This section aims to assist you in becoming a proficient smartphone photographer. These pointers and techniques will enable you to capture moments with grace and originality, regardless of your level of experience with photography or your level of familiarity with the realm of visual storytelling.

1. Recognizing Different Camera Modes
Explore the multitude of camera settings on your Galaxy S24 Ultra. Every mode has a distinct function, from Night Mode for low-light brightness to Pro Mode for customised settings. Investigate and test to find the best mode for each shooting situation.

2. Leveraging AI's Power
Your photography helper is the Galaxy S24 Ultra's AI capabilities. Give AI the freedom to examine scenarios and adjust parameters to provide the best outcomes. Allow the intelligence of your smartphone to improve your photos, from subject recognition to exposure adjustments.

3. Improving Techniques for Composition
For photos to be appealing, composition is essential. Acquire and use basic composition principles, including symmetry, leading lines, and the rule of thirds. By arranging things in a manner that draws the viewer in, you may improve the look of your images.

4. Making the Most of Zoom Features

Make the most of the remarkable zoom powers of the Galaxy S24 Ultra. Try using an optical zoom to get clear and sharp magnification. Utilise the Macro Lens to capture unique close-ups, and explore the artistic possibilities of the Periscope Telephoto Lens.

5. Adopting a Nighttime Photography Style

The Galaxy S24 Ultra's Night Mode turns dimly lit settings into breathtaking works of art. Learn how to use this function so that you can take clear, detailed pictures even in low light. To get the ideal nighttime photo, change the exposure settings.

6. Opening the Manual Control Pro Mode

Pro Mode is your entry point if you want total control over your photographs. To fit your artistic vision into every photo, play around with parameters like ISO, shutter speed, and white balance. Pro Mode provides a platform for photographers to showcase their own aesthetic.

7. Becoming an Expert in Portraiture

The Galaxy S24 Ultra's strong optics and DepthVision Sensor make it a remarkable tool for portrait shooting. Try out the portrait and Live Focus settings to get superb background blur in your professional-looking portraits.

8. Examining Effects and Filters

By experimenting with the many filters and effects available, you may increase your creativity. Use filters to give your images a unique look that might range from retro to modern. Try using selective colour and bokeh techniques to add creative flare.

9. Sorting and Saving Pictures

Remain structured while you take a wealth of memories. Make use of the Gallery app to organise your pictures into albums. For extra piece of mind, regularly backup your priceless memories to Samsung Cloud or other cloud storage services.

10. Ongoing Education and Trial and error

The field of photography is always changing. Remain inquisitive and receptive to picking up new skills. Try varying the topics, locations, and viewpoints to keep your abilities sharp. You may express your creativity with the Galaxy S24 Ultra.

Exploring Advanced Camera Modes and Features

Greetings from the realm of your Samsung Galaxy S24 Ultra's sophisticated camera settings and functions. We explore the advanced features that enhance your photographic experience in this part. Visual storytelling may take on new dimensions as you explore these advanced tools, regardless of your level of expertise.

1. Mastering Pro Mode: Accuracy at Your Fingertips

Your entryway to manual control is Pro Mode, which lets you adjust parameters like an experienced photographer. Explore adjusting the ISO, regulating the shutter speed, and adjusting the white balance to take pictures with unmatched accuracy. Pro Mode gives you total control over how you express your ideas.

2. One Shot: Sum Up the Big Ideas in a Blink
Singular Take makes catching the ideal photo less difficult. Your Galaxy S24 Ultra uses many lenses and settings with only one shutter push to take a wide range of pictures and movies. With Single Take, you can capture amazing stills and dynamic films without ever missing a moment.

3. The Director's Perspective: Multilens Cinematic Magnificence
With Director's View, you can unleash your inner filmmaker. Easily transition between lenses while filming to get various viewpoints in a single clip. This function is ideal for producing dynamic and interesting material, such as visual narratives or event documentation.

4. Time-bending Creativity with Super Slow-Mo and Hyperlapse
Use Super Slow-Mo and Hyperlapse to transform everyday situations into breathtaking scenes. Make fascinating hyperlapse films by condensing time or capturing intriguing slow-motion videos. These elements give your visual storytelling repertoire a dash of magical cinema.

5. Night Hyperlapse: Using Light to Paint Nightscapes
Use Night Hyperlapse to elevate Hyperlapse to a new level. With the help of this function, you may produce beautiful

time-lapse films in dim lighting. With the help of this creative and alluring option, capture the spirit of lively cityscapes or calm starry sky.

6. Video Recording of Professional Quality

Your Galaxy S24 Ultra is a professional-calibre video recorder as well as a still photography powerhouse. Capture films at 8K resolution for unmatched detail and clarity. Utilise sophisticated video functions, including manual focus, to use your smartphone to create breathtaking tales.

7. Video Portrait: Dramatic Emphasis on the Subject

Use the Portrait Video option to enhance your video portraits. With the help of this function, the backdrop will have a subtle bokeh effect that makes your subject stand out. Easily record polished-looking video footage to enhance the interest and allure of your visual storytelling.

8. AI-Powered Scene Identification: Astute Photography Support

Give your Galaxy S24 Ultra's AI-based Scene Recognition a chance to examine scenes. This tool optimises your photographs for optimal outcomes by automatically adjusting camera settings depending on the identified scenario. Allow the intelligence of the gadget to improve your photography, whether it be for landscapes or portraits.

9. Studio-Grade Audio Recording with Multiple Mics

Make sure the audio in your videos matches their stunning visuals by using Multi-Mic Recording. With the ability to record from several microphones at once, the Galaxy S24

Ultra can produce studio-calibre audio. With this function, you may film vlogs or capture live performances and still get crystal-clear audio.

10. Fun Features and AR Doodle: Bringing Playfulness to Creativity
Use AR Doodle and other entertaining features to add a lighthearted touch to your pictures and movies. In real time, create, animate, and engage with your creations. These elements provide your visual material an extra creative and entertaining touch, increasing its personalization and engagement.

Throughout the process of using these sophisticated camera settings and functions, keep in mind that the Galaxy S24 Ultra is an incredible creative tool. Push the limits of your photography adventure by experimenting and exploring. Your smartphone has all the tools it needs to make every moment a work of art, from fun augmented reality features to high-quality films.

Chapter 5

Processing Powerhouse

Introducing the brains behind the Samsung Galaxy S24 Ultra: a powerful processor that guarantees smooth multitasking, quick performance, and unmatched efficiency. This chapter explores the state-of-the-art technology that elevates your smartphone to a new level of performance and responsiveness.

1. Unmatched Performance: Exynos 2200 or Snapdragon 8cx

Depending on your area, the Exynos 2200 or Snapdragon 8cx is the processor at the heart of the Galaxy S24 Ultra. With their unwavering speed and efficiency, these processors are designed to make sure that your smartphone can easily perform any work. Experience unparalleled performance for everything from long gaming sessions to mobile productivity.

2. Enough RAM - Your Passport to Expert Multitasking

Managing many tasks at once is made easier by the generous RAM on your Galaxy S24 Ultra. A seamless and responsive user experience is delivered by your device's ability to smoothly switch between applications thanks to setups that provide up to 12GB or more. Immerse yourself in seamless multitasking like never before with no more delays or distractions.

3. UFS 3.1 Storage – Lightning-Quick Access to Data

For speedy access to your data, applications, and video, storage speed is essential. With its UFS 3.1 storage system, the Galaxy S24 Ultra offers lightning-fast read and write rates. The speed at which your smartphone reacts when you launch applications, transfer data, or take high-quality images adds to the seamless user experience.

4. Mali-G78 or Adreno GPU Enhanced Graphics

Use the Adreno GPU (graphics processing unit) or Mali-G78 to improve your multimedia and gaming experiences. These GPUs provide excellent graphics, fluid gameplay, and effective rendering. Your Galaxy S24 Ultra is capable of handling graphically demanding apps and engaging in visually stimulating games.

5. Sustained Peak Performance - Optimised Cooling System

Even very intensive activities might produce heat, the Galaxy S24 Ultra has a cooling mechanism that is geared to mitigate this. No matter how long you play games or use resource-intensive apps, the cooling system keeps your device running at optimal performance without sacrificing efficiency or temperature.

6. Performance Management Assisted by AI

Artificial intelligence is used by your Galaxy S24 Ultra to improve performance management. Based on your use habits, the gadget automatically distributes resources to maximise effectiveness and minimise energy consumption. With the help of artificial intelligence, your smartphone will be able to adjust to your demands and provide you a tailored and responsive experience.

7. 5G Connectivity: Redefining Connectivity and Speed

Discover the next level of connection with 5G features. Low latency, improved connection, and very quick download and upload speeds are all made possible with your Galaxy S24 Ultra. 5G connectivity guarantees a quick and dependable connection whether you're downloading big files, taking part in video conversations, or streaming high-definition entertainment.

8. Long-lasting Power via Battery Management

Your Galaxy S24 Ultra optimises energy usage by combining strong performance with effective battery management. Your device's variable refresh rate and clever power-saving technologies guarantee a long battery life, allowing you to stay connected without sacrificing performance throughout the day.

9. UI Improvements - Simplified User Interface

Your Galaxy S24 Ultra's powerful processing capabilities along with the user-friendly One UI provide a fluidly integrated experience. One UI enhances the device's processing power, enabling responsiveness with every touch and swipe, from seamless navigation to improved app interactions.

10. An Evolutionary Device: Future-Ready Processing

Your Galaxy S24 Ultra is a powerful, future-ready gadget, not simply a gadget. With its advanced processing technology, your smartphone is ready to handle the rigours of the new and innovative apps of the future. With a gadget that changes with you, you can stay ahead of the curve.

Enjoy the speed, efficiency, and innovation that characterise the heart of this incredible smartphone as you investigate the computing powerhouse that is Samsung Galaxy S24 Ultra. Your smartphone is designed to improve every facet of your digital experience, from fluid multitasking to high-performance gaming.

Unleashing the Performance: Processor and RAM

- Embark on an unparalleled performance journey with the Samsung Galaxy S24 Ultra. This section delves into the scientific wonders that comprise your device's CPU and RAM, which act as its beating heart. Together, these two essential elements provide lightning-fast response, fluid multitasking, and an overall unmatched user experience.

1. The Exynos 2200 or Snapdragon 8cx, the Powerhouse CPU

A state-of-the-art CPU, the Exynos 2200 or Snapdragon 8cx, depending on your location, powers the Galaxy S24 Ultra. These processors are designed with great care to provide powerful performance that goes above and beyond. Your smartphone performs activities that need a lot of resources and quick app launches with amazing efficiency.

2. Plenty of RAM for Expert Multitasking

The large RAM capacity of the Galaxy S24 Ultra allows for unprecedented levels of multitasking. Your smartphone can easily handle many apps at once with setups that provide up to 12GB or more, making for a snappy and responsive user experience. Say goodbye to lags and delays; your smartphone is a superb multitasking partner.

3. Lightning-fast data access with UFS 3.1 storage

With UFS 3.1 storage technology, the Galaxy S24 Ultra distinguishes itself in the world of fast data access. This guarantees blazingly fast read and write rates, which translates to rapid file transfers, program launches, and a snappy user experience all around. Bid adieu to ineffective performance and welcome to efficiency.

4. Mali-G78 or Adreno GPU-Enhanced Graphics

With the Mali-G78 or Adreno GPU, you can improve graphics performance for entertainment, gaming, and other applications. Every on-screen moment is a visual joy because of the gorgeous images, fluid animations, and effective rendering that the Galaxy S24 Ultra offers.

5. A Better Cooling System for Long-Term Functioning

Work that requires a lot of energy produces heat, yet your Galaxy S24 Ultra has an efficient cooling system. This guarantees continued optimal performance without sacrificing device temperature or efficiency. Your smartphone remains cool whether you're playing games or using resource-intensive apps.

6. Performance Management Assisted by AI

The integration of artificial intelligence is crucial in improving performance management. Based on your use habits, Samsung Galaxy S24 Ultra smartly distributes resources to maximise effectiveness and minimise battery consumption. By adjusting to your demands, the gadget offers a responsive and customised experience.

7. Redefining Speed with 5G Connectivity

With 5G connection on your Galaxy S24 Ultra, you can go into the future. Take advantage of improved connection, reduced latency, and very fast download and upload rates. 5G guarantees a fast and dependable connection whether you're downloading huge files, engaging in video chats, or streaming high-definition entertainment.

8. Maintaining Power via Battery Management

The energy consumption of your Galaxy S24 Ultra is optimised by balancing power and efficiency. The gadget guarantees an extended battery life with features like an adjustable refresh rate and sophisticated power-saving measures. Maintain connectivity without sacrificing effectiveness throughout the day.

9. Seamless Integration: One UI Enhancements

The user-friendly One UI completes the picture by adding to the processing power. Reactivity is ensured in every connection with your smartphone via seamless navigation, improved app interactions, and an intuitive UI.

10. A Device that Evolves: Future-Ready Processing
Your Galaxy S24 Ultra is a powerful, future-ready device, not simply a smartphone. With its state-of-the-art processing technology, your device is ready to handle the rigours of the innovations and applications of the future. With a gadget that changes with you, you can stay ahead of the curve.

Multitasking Like a Pro

Learn to multitask so that you can get the most out of your Samsung Galaxy S24 Ultra. Your smartphone's strong CPU, generous RAM, and user-friendly UI enable you to multitask with ease. We'll walk you through the features and methods in this part to help you multitask like a master.

1. Pairing Apps: Easy Side-by-Side Communication
Your Galaxy S24 Ultra's ability to operate two applications at once with App Pairing is one of its most impressive features. You may launch commonly used app pairings in split-screen mode by customising their launchers. App Pairing makes multitasking easier, whether you're taking notes in a conference or talking while viewing a video.

2. Split-Screen Perspective: Optimising Screen Area
To split your screen between two applications of your choosing, activate Split-Screen View. When you need to consult data from one app while working in another, this capability comes in quite helpful. Swipe from the right or left

side of the screen to activate, then choose the first app to occupy the available space, followed by the second app.

3. Floating Apps for Quick Access in Pop-up View

With Pop-up View, you can multitask more effectively by enabling certain programs to float on top of others. Just picture being able to reply to a message without ever having to leave the program you're using. To arrange the program window where you find it most comfortable, just touch and drag it. It's seamless multitasking.

4. Edge Panels: Instant App Access Right Now

Edge Panels are a group of quick-access shortcuts, applications, and features that appear when you swipe in from the edge of your screen. To maximise the effectiveness of your multitasking efforts, personalise these panels with the programs you use most often. Your favourite applications are now a swipe away with Edge Panels.

5. Floating Applications: Enduring Efficiency

Some programs have the ability to become floating icons, which let them float above other apps. For continuous operations like messages or calculating, this capability is ideal. Navigating among different programs may be done with uninterrupted productivity if you enable Floating Apps in your settings.

6. Smooth Transitions Across Devices: Application Continuity

Use App Continuity if you own numerous Samsung devices to ensure a smooth task transfer. Launch an application on your

Galaxy S24 Ultra, then use a compatible tablet or another Samsung device to seamlessly carry on with it. Your gadgets work together harmoniously to provide a multitasking ecology.

7. Fast Switch: Simple Application Navigation
With Quick Switch, switching between frequently used applications is a snap. The navigation bar allows you to swipe left or right to move between the two applications that you last used. The ability to switch between activities quickly and easily without having to go back to the home screen is made possible by this simple action.

8. Task Manager: Customise Your Environment for Multitasking
To examine and control the programs that are open, use the Task Manager. To access the Task Manager, swipe up from the bottom of the screen, then pause. You may ensure maximum performance and free up resources for your ongoing work by closing superfluous programs here.

9. Divided Audio: Continuous Sound Experience
With Split Sound, you may choose distinct audio sources for each program in split-screen mode, resulting in a smooth audio experience. To create a customised and engaging multitasking environment, play music on one side and watch a video on the other.

10. Quick Tips for Multitasking: Increasing Productivity
Investigate different gestures and shortcuts to improve the effectiveness of your multitasking. To adjust the multitasking

experience to your liking, the Galaxy S24 Ultra provides a variety of choices, ranging from three-finger gestures to custom gestures inside your settings.

Getting the hang of multitasking on your Samsung Galaxy S24 Ultra may lead to new levels of ease and productivity. With these tools at your disposal, you can maximise your productivity, move between projects with ease, and use the full potential of your state-of-the-art smartphone.

Gaming on the Galaxy S24 Ultra: A Seamless Experience

- Discover an unmatched gaming experience with your Samsung Galaxy S24 Ultra

Your smartphone becomes a powerful gaming machine with cutting-edge technology and cutting-edge features, providing a fluid and immersive gaming experience. We'll explore the Galaxy S24 Ultra's gaming skills in this part, offering you features, improvements, and advice to improve your gaming experiences.

1. Dynamic Display: Eye-Catching Visual Appeal for Gamers

The Dynamic Display of the Galaxy S24 Ultra has a fast refresh rate, brilliant colours, and HDR compatibility. Immerse yourself in games with gorgeous graphics, fluid animations, and a touch screen that responds. Your games' demands are met by the Dynamic Display, which makes sure every detail is vibrant and every movement is smooth.

2. Game Booster: Get the Best Performance Right Now

When playing games, turn on Game Booster to fully use your device's capabilities. This function creates a focused gameplay experience by streamlining operations, distributing resources effectively, and reducing distractions. For a customised gaming experience, use the Quick Settings panel or your settings to access Game Booster.

3. Cooling System: Play Hard Without Getting Hot
Play for longer periods of time without fear of overheating. A sophisticated cooling mechanism on the Galaxy S24 Ultra controls the device's temperature during prolonged gaming sessions. This guarantees that your gadget remains cool and continues to operate at its best for longer periods of time.

4. Expert-Level Controls: Accuracy at Your Points of Contact
Take full use of pro-grade controllers that are snappy and precise while playing games. Whether you're playing fast-paced action games or exploring virtual worlds, the Galaxy S24 Ultra's adjustable settings, snappy touch screen, and tactile buttons provide for an enhanced gaming experience.

5. Dolby Atmos: Virtual Reality Sound for Virtual Realism
Use Dolby Atmos to improve the audio quality of your games, with surround sound that envelops you. Dolby Atmos enhances the realism of your gaming experience by adding sounds such as distant thunderclaps and footsteps coming from behind, elevating it to new levels.

6. Extended Gaming Sessions Due to Large Battery Capacity

Take pleasure in prolonged gaming sessions without worrying about battery life. With the Galaxy S24 Ultra, you can play games for hours on end because of its huge battery capacity. Effective power management allows you to concentrate on the game uninterrupted.

7. Record Your Games: Share and Capture Your Victories

Easily capture and distribute your game victories. With the built-in game recording function of the Galaxy S24 Ultra, you may record gameplay. Show off your prowess in style by sharing your finest moments, tactics, and wins with friends and the gaming community.

8. Customise Your Setup: Compatible with Gaming Accessory

Examine a selection of Galaxy S24 Ultra-compatible gaming peripherals. Controllers and audio accessories.

Chapter 6

Connectivity and Network

Master the sophisticated networking and connection options of your Samsung Galaxy S24 Ultra to realise its full potential. We'll walk you through configuring and optimising your device in this part so that sharing, quick internet access, and smooth communication are all possible. Upgrade your experience with connection by using the Galaxy S24 Ultra.

1. Extremely Fast Internet Speeds with 5G Connectivity
Dive yourself into the 5G future of lightning-fast internet access. With 5G network compatibility, the Galaxy S24 Ultra offers blazingly quick downloads, lag-free streaming, and a flawless online experience. Experience the power of next-gen connectivity in the palm of your hand.

2. Improved Wireless Performance with Wi-Fi 6E

Use Wi-Fi 6E technology to improve the performance of your wireless network. Connect to Wi-Fi networks more quickly, effectively, and extensively. Wi-Fi 6E offers a dependable and fast connection, ideal for online gaming or streaming high definition media.

3. Bluetooth 5.2: Easily Pairing Devices
Easily connect and share using Bluetooth 5.2. Experience dependable and quick connections with wearables, speakers,

headphones, and other connected devices. With its cutting-edge Bluetooth technology, the Galaxy S24 Ultra guarantees a flawless pairing experience for all of your wireless gadgets.

4. Transactions are Fast and Simple with NFC Technology
Use NFC (Near Field Communication) to facilitate fast and simple transactions. Utilise your Galaxy S24 Ultra for tickets, contactless payments, and other functions. The NFC capabilities of the smartphone provide a plethora of opportunities for quick and safe interactions.

5. Data Transfer and Charging Versatile with USB Type-C
Accept USB Type-C's ease of use for flexible data transmission and charging. A USB Type-C connector on the Galaxy S24 Ultra enables quick charging and effective data transmission between your mobile and other compatible devices. Experience the advantages of a universal connection by connecting with ease.

6. Mobile Hotspot: Distribute Your Link
Convert your Galaxy S24 Ultra into a portable hotspot so that other devices may access your internet. The mobile hotspot function makes sure you remain connected, even while you're out and about or in a place with poor internet service. It also enables other devices to connect to the internet via your smartphone.

7. Optimising Network Settings: Customising to Meet Your Requirements

Use the network options on the Galaxy S24 Ultra to personalise and enhance your connection. To fit your demands, change the roaming, network, and data consumption settings. Customise the connection settings on your device to get the best possible experience.

8. Double SIM Functionality: Harmonize Professional and Personal Life

Benefit from the dual SIM feature of the Galaxy S24 Ultra for a flexible communication experience. Easily swap between SIM cards, manage personal and business lines on the same device, and maintain connectivity whenever and whenever you want. The ability to use two SIM cards gives you more options for communication.

9. Troubleshooting Connectivity: Fast Solutions for Typical Problems

Have problems with connectivity? Do not be alarmed. Quick troubleshooting guides for typical connection problems are provided in this area. Discover how to quickly fix problems, from Bluetooth kinks to Wi-Fi snags, to guarantee a stable connection.

10. Protecting Your Connectivity with Data Security and Privacy

Examine the options and features pertaining to privacy and data security. Make sure your connection is safe and quick at the same time. With its secured connections and privacy settings, the Galaxy S24 Ultra puts your data security first, giving you piece of mind.

  With the Samsung Galaxy S24 Ultra, you can become an expert at connecting. Whether you're using Bluetooth to pair devices with ease, enjoying the speed of 5G, or adjusting network settings, this chapter gives you the expertise to take full use of your device's networking capabilities. With the Galaxy S24 Ultra, you can simply share content, stay connected, and have new levels of communication.

Embracing the Era of 5G: High-Speed Connectivity

Introducing the Samsung Galaxy S24 Ultra—welcome to the connection of the future. This section will examine how 5G technology changes your mobile experience and dig into the exciting world of this cutting-edge technology. Prepare to welcome the 5G era, when fast internet becomes a game-changer rather than just a perk.

1. Unlocking Record-Breaking Speeds

Get ready to be astounded by the very quick speeds that 5G offers for your Galaxy S24 Ultra. You're not simply accessing the internet when you have 5G connectivity—you're using it at previously unheard-of speeds. 5G guarantees a smooth and quick experience whether you're downloading big files, playing online games, or streaming high-definition video.

2. Smooth Gaming and Streaming

Lag and buffering are gone. The very low latency of 5G guarantees continuous and seamless gaming and streaming experiences. Enjoy responsive online gaming and top-notch video streaming while using all of the Galaxy S24 Ultra's potent features.

3. Instant Uploads, Quicker Downloads
Uploading and downloading have never gone so quickly. 5G technology transforms data transport, making it possible to post material instantaneously and download big files in a flash. Your digital interactions are accelerated with the Galaxy S24 Ultra's 5G connection, whether you're sharing media, updating documents, or working together in real time.

4. Modern Lifestyle: Enhanced Connectivity
Take advantage of connections that adapt to your busy schedule. 5G makes sure your Galaxy S24 Ultra stays connected and responsive whether you're working from a distance, traversing congested city streets, or visiting new locations. Follow your path and continue to be productive wherever it leads.

5. Leveraging IoT Potential
The Galaxy S24 Ultra has 5G connection, allowing you to enter the Internet of Things (IoT) age. Easily connect and manage all of your smart devices, including wearable technology and smart household appliances. With the powerful 5G network, your gadget may serve as the focal point of your networked digital world.

6. Communication's Future

5G is about rethinking communication, not simply about speed. Take advantage of realistic virtual meetings, lag-free audio conversations, and crystal-clear video conferences. The 5G capabilities of the Galaxy S24 Ultra take communication to the next level and guarantee that you always have a clear and precise connection.

7. Getting Around in the 5G Environment

Recognize the subtleties of 5G connection and its workings. This section offers guidance on navigating the 5G environment, including topics such as coverage concerns and various frequency bands. Arm yourself with information to maximise the 5G capabilities of the Galaxy S24 Ultra in a range of situations and places.

8. Tailoring 5G Configurations to Your Requirements

Tailor your 5G experience to your requirements and tastes. Examine the Galaxy S24 Ultra's 5G connection settings, which include choices for network preferences, data use, and other areas. Customise the device to meet your specific connection needs, and take advantage of a tailored 5G experience.

Take advantage of the Samsung Galaxy S24 Ultra to welcome the 5G age. This chapter has shown you how high-speed connection can change everything about how you interact with the digital world. 5G on the Galaxy S24 Ultra is not just a feature—it's a revolutionary step into the future of mobile connection, offering quicker downloads and flawless streaming. Prepare to connect, explore, and take advantage of 5G's unparalleled power.

Wi-Fi, Bluetooth, and NFC: Seamless Connectivity Options

Welcome to the Samsung Galaxy S24 Ultra's world of flawless connection. We'll look at the flexible connection choices outside of standard cellular networks in this chapter. With features like high-speed Wi-Fi, Bluetooth for convenience, and NFC magic, the Galaxy S24 Ultra makes sure you're always connected. Now let's explore the world of wireless connection choices that improve your experience with smartphones.

1. Fast Wi-Fi Accessibility

With the enhanced Wi-Fi features of the Galaxy S24 Ultra, enjoy dependable and quick internet connections. Connect to accessible Wi-Fi networks with ease, whether you're at home, at a café, or at the workplace. Learn how to manage network preferences, optimise Wi-Fi settings, and guarantee a seamless surfing experience.

2. Bluetooth: Easily Linking Devices

Discover the possibilities of Bluetooth connections for wireless devices with the Galaxy S24 Ultra. Connect your smartphone to a wide variety of Bluetooth-capable gadgets, such as fitness trackers, smartwatches, headphones, and speakers. This section offers tips and tricks for pairing, controlling connections, and resolving Bluetooth-related problems.

3. Tap, Share, and Pay with NFC Magic

With the Galaxy S24 Ultra, discover the miracle of Near Field Communication (NFC). NFC facilitates easy communication by letting you exchange contacts, data, and images with only a touch. Use Samsung Pay and other NFC-enabled payment options to explore the world of contactless payments. Discover how to use NFC to its fullest for safe and easy transactions.

4. Two SIM Slots for Better Connectivity

Explore the benefits of the Galaxy S24 Ultra's dual SIM functionality. Dual SIM capability offers versatility and convenience whether you're juggling business and personal numbers or looking into affordable roaming choices while on the go. Discover how to configure and maintain two SIM cards for the best possible connection.

5. Using Smart Switches to Improve Connectivity

With Smart Switch, switching from an older handset to the Galaxy S24 Ultra is now simpler than ever. You may easily move stuff from your old smartphone to the new one thanks to this capability. Discover how to use Smart Switch step-by-step to ensure a seamless shift without losing crucial data.

6. GPS and Location-Based Services

Discover the full potential of your Galaxy S24 Ultra's global positioning system (GPS) and location-based services. This section explains how to use location services efficiently, from navigating new streets to finding local areas of interest. To ensure a safe and customised experience, be aware of privacy settings and make the most of location-based services.

7. Customization and Connectivity Settings

Customise your connection settings to save battery life and your preferences. Enter the Galaxy S24 Ultra's settings to see whether Wi-Fi, Bluetooth, NFC, and other features are available. Discover how to adjust connection settings to better suit your use habits and increase the device's overall effectiveness.

8. Resolving Problems with Connectivity

Having problems with connectivity? For typical problems with Wi-Fi, Bluetooth, and NFC, this section offers answers and troubleshooting advice. Gain the skills necessary to handle connectivity problems on your own, whether they are related to a lost Bluetooth connection or trouble connecting to a Wi-Fi network.

Take use of the Samsung Galaxy S24 Ultra to live a connected lifestyle. This chapter has unveiled the variety of connectivity choices available to you, including smooth Bluetooth connections, fast Wi-Fi, and the power of NFC. The seamless connectivity in the digital world is guaranteed with the Galaxy S24 Ultra, whether you're sharing, streaming, or navigating.

Mobile Hotspot and Tethering: Sharing Your Connection

We'll explore the potent capabilities of tethering and mobile hotspot on the Samsung Galaxy S24 Ultra in this section. You can easily share your internet connection with other devices by turning your smartphone into a portable Wi-Fi hub. With the flexibility and convenience of mobile hotspot and tethering offered by the Galaxy S24 Ultra, you can connect your laptop or tablet even while you're on the road.

1. Mobile Hotspot: Your Portable Wi-Fi Center
The mobile hotspot function on the Galaxy S24 Ultra allows you to create your own Wi-Fi network wherever you are, giving you independence. An instruction manual for configuring and turning on your mobile hotspot may be found in this section. Discover how to customise your hotspot experience using network name and password settings, among other choices, to make it safe and unique.

2. Tethering: USB or Bluetooth Device Connection
By connecting your Galaxy S24 Ultra to other devices via Bluetooth or USB, you may increase the functionality of your connection. Tethering increases your connectivity possibilities, whether you're using it to share data across devices or connect your laptop for a reliable internet connection. Examine the tethering configuration procedure and learn how to create tethered connections that are effective and trouble-free.

3. Controlling Data Usage and Connected Devices

Learn how to monitor data use and manage devices that are connected to your mobile hotspot. With the Galaxy S24 Ultra, you can monitor which apps use the most data, set data use limitations, and check connected devices. You may prevent unforeseen data costs and maintain control over your shared connection with the help of this section.

4. Improving Tethering and Hotspot Configurations

Adjust the tethering and mobile hotspot settings to suit your needs and save battery life. Examine the advanced options, which include automated hotspot turnoff, connection timeout, and other features. For a smooth and effective experience, find out how to balance sharing your connection with protecting your device's resources.

5. Fixing Problems with Tethering and Hotspot

Having trouble connecting to your tether or mobile hotspot? For typical problems, this section offers answers and troubleshooting advice. Gain the ability to properly handle and fix hotspot and tethering difficulties, from connection dropouts to compatibility concerns.

6. Precautionary Steps to Take When Sharing Connections

Use recommended methods for tethering and mobile hotspot to protect your shared connection. Find more about password strength, encryption choices, and other security steps to keep unwanted users from accessing your connection. You will learn how to create a dependable and safe shared connection in this part.

Discover the Samsung Galaxy S24 Ultra's tethering and mobile hotspot capabilities. These capabilities allow you the ease and flexibility you want in a variety of scenarios, whether you're sharing your internet connection with friends, coworkers, or other devices. This chapter gives you the expertise to maximise your Galaxy S24 Ultra's mobile hotspot and tethering features, from setup to troubleshooting.

Chapter 7

Software Harmony

We will examine the Samsung Galaxy S24 Ultra's complex software environment in this chapter, emphasising its user-friendly UI, robust apps, and the smooth incorporation of cutting-edge technologies. Learn more about the software elements that make up the harmony of your smartphone experience as a whole.

1. Intuitive Simplicity: A Single UI for Navigation
Explore the Samsung Galaxy S24 Ultra's One UI, which has an intuitive design. This section walks you through One UI's customization, personalization, and navigation features. Discover how to take full use of its user-friendly design to guarantee a seamless and pleasurable experience with your gadget.

2. Bixby: The Smart Virtual Helper
Discover everything that the Galaxy S24 Ultra's intelligent virtual assistant, Bixby, has to offer. Discover Bixby's potential and incorporate it into your everyday routine to take use of its voice commands and predictive suggestion features. This section offers guidance on configuring and refining Bixby to provide a customised and effective user experience.

3. App Ecosystem: Examining Downloadable and Pre-installed Applications

Explore the wide range of apps that the Galaxy S24 Ultra has to offer. Learn how to use the applications that come pre-installed and get suggestions for more apps that will improve your smartphone experience. This section assists you in choosing a set of applications that are suitable for your requirements, regardless of whether your priorities are creativity, productivity, or amusement.

4. Software Upgrades: Guaranteeing Optimal Efficiency

Examine the software update procedure to stay up to speed on the newest features, security advancements, and upgrades. This section explains how to check for updates, read release notes, and make sure you have the most recent software upgrades installed on your Galaxy S24 Ultra to maximise performance.

5. Themes and Customization: Personalised Device Experience

Customise and personalise your Galaxy S24 Ultra with a wide range of themes and customization choices. This section explains how to alter themes, backgrounds, and icon styles to suit your own tastes. Use your imagination to create a smartphone that accurately captures your own flair.

6. Security Elements: Protecting Your Online Image

Examine the security precautions that the Galaxy S24 Ultra's OS has built in. To safeguard your sensitive data, find out about secure folder features, biometric authentication, and other security measures. You are now able to take charge of your online privacy and security thanks to this area.

7. Inclusive Design for All Users: Accessibility Features

Discover the features that make the Galaxy S24 Ultra user-friendly for everybody by exploring its accessibility features. This section offers an overview of features that guarantee an inclusive experience for users with a variety of requirements, from hearing assistance to vision upgrades.

With confidence, navigate the Samsung Galaxy S24 Ultra's software environment. This chapter provides you with the information to fully use the software harmony on your Galaxy S24 Ultra, whether you're personalising your smartphone, keeping up with the newest features, or protecting your online reputation.

Intelligent User Experience: AI Integrations

Venture into the world of Artificial Intelligence (AI) integrations that improve the Samsung Galaxy S24 Ultra user experience. We'll explore the clever features and functions driven by AI in this area, which will improve the general convenience and usage of your smartphone.

1. AI for Photography: Enhancement and Scene Recognition

Watch how AI works in tandem with the Galaxy S24 Ultra's camera system to demonstrate its brilliance. Discover how your photography is optimised with AI-driven scene recognition, which modifies settings automatically according to the subject and environment. Discover the subtleties of

AI-powered improvements that improve the photographed moments' visual attractiveness.

2. Typing and Predictive Text: An Intelligent Keyboard Experience

With the Galaxy S24 Ultra's predictive text and typing functions, you may experience the effectiveness of AI in text input. Discover how the gadget anticipates your next word, adjusts to your writing style, and makes intelligent recommendations to help you communicate more efficiently and type less. The AI-driven intelligence that powers a flawless keyboard experience is revealed in this section.

3. Voice Commands Assisted by AI: Bixby's Development

Examine the development of Samsung's virtual assistant, Bixby, and how it combines AI-assisted voice requests. Examine how Bixby uses AI to carry out tasks, comprehend natural language, and provide tailored suggestions. This section walks you through using voice-activated AI to interact with your smartphone in an easy-to-use and hands-free manner.

4. Intelligent Battery Management: Enhancing Power Utilisation

Discover how AI can effectively manage the battery life of your smartphone. Discover how the Galaxy S24 Ultra analyses your use habits and optimises battery consumption with the help of AI algorithms. Learn about the features that guarantee your smartphone lasts longer between charges by exploring adaptive power-saving capabilities.

5. AI-Powered Personalization: Customization Suggestions

Learn how AI adapts content suggestions and recommendations to your preferences and use habits. This section examines how the Galaxy S24 Ultra adjusts to your behaviours to provide a tailored and pleasurable user experience, from app suggestions to personalised content streams.

6. AI in Security: Improvements via Biometrics

Examine how AI and biometric identification may be used to improve security on the Galaxy S24 Ultra. Find out how AI helps with fingerprint scanning, face recognition, and other biometric security capabilities so that your device and personal information are intelligently and robustly protected.

Embrace the smarter user experiences of the future with the Samsung Galaxy S24 Ultra's AI integrations. AI has a major impact on how intelligent, simple, and personalised your smartphone interactions can be—whether it's via photo revolutionization, battery life optimization, or personalised suggestions.

Personalising Your Device: Themes and Settings

Explore the many ways you can customise your Samsung Galaxy S24 Ultra to fit your own style and tastes as we dive into the world of personalization. This section reveals the wide range of customization choices at your disposal, from themes that change the device's appearance and feel to complex settings that meet your unique requirements.

1. Changing Aesthetics: Dynamic Themes

Learn how dynamic themes, as opposed to static backgrounds, may have great impact. Discover how dynamic themes that change depending on the time of day or your location may help you customise your Galaxy S24 Ultra. Explore a world where the look of your smartphone changes to fit various settings and emotions.

2. Customization and Icon Packs: Creating a Special Interface

Investigate the wide range of icon packs and modification possibilities to let your imagination run wild. Discover how to update your home screen with distinctive widgets, fonts, and icons to create a customised interface that expresses your own style. This section walks you through the process of customising every element of your device's appearance.

3. A Visual Odyssey with the Wallpaper Carousel

Use the Wallpaper Carousel function to go on a visual adventure. Learn how the Galaxy S24 Ultra updates your home screen automatically with carefully chosen wallpapers. Examine the modification options to choose your own photographs or choose to have the gadget automatically update its wallpaper every day.

4. Mastering Dark Mode: Elegant and Power-Saving

Delve into the gorgeous realm of Dark Mode and its dual advantages. Find out how to activate this function for a stylish and battery-saving interface that lessens eye strain in dimly lit areas. This section offers guidance on adjusting the settings for Dark Mode and smoothly incorporating it into your regular use.

5. Customising Visuals with Enhanced Display Settings

Utilise advanced options to fully realise the possibilities of display customisation. Examine choices for adjusting resolution, screen brightness, and colour profiles to customise images to your taste. Learn how you may customise a viewing experience with the Galaxy S24 Ultra to fit your own visual preferences.

6. Inclusive Personalization: Accessibility Settings

Examine the accessibility settings on your gadget to ensure that everyone can use it. This section walks you through the inclusive customisation choices that guarantee a smooth and pleasant experience for users with a variety of requirements, from font modifications to screen readers.

7. Intuitive User Interface Tailoring: One UI Customization

Give yourself up to One UI's straightforward customization options. Discover how to utilise the features and options to customise the user interface to your tastes and workflow. An extensive tutorial on customising One UI to be completely yours may be found in this section.

Make your Samsung Galaxy S24 Ultra uniquely yours by customising it to reflect your unique style. Customization options abound, ranging from dynamic themes that adjust to your surroundings to intricate settings that satisfy specific tastes. This area gives you the tools to turn your gadget into a really one-of-a-kind and customised friend.

Conclusion

Maximising Your Samsung Galaxy S24 Ultra Experience

As we conclude this comprehensive guide to the Samsung Galaxy S24 Ultra, you are now equipped with the knowledge to unlock the full potential of your extraordinary device. The journey through the intricacies of its features, settings, and capabilities has laid the foundation for an unparalleled smartphone experience. Let's recap the key takeaways and explore how to stay updated on additional resources.

1. Unleashing the Power Within

The Samsung Galaxy S24 Ultra is not just a smartphone; it's a powerhouse of innovation and cutting-edge technology. From the dynamic display to the revolutionary camera system, every aspect of this device has been meticulously crafted to elevate your smartphone experience. As you navigate through its features, remember that the true potential lies in your hands. Experiment, explore, and make the Galaxy S24 Ultra uniquely yours.

2. Mastering Security and Biometrics

In the realm of security, the Galaxy S24 Ultra stands as a fortress. The biometric marvels of facial recognition and the ultrasonic fingerprint scanner ensure that your device is not only secure but also easily accessible. The Knox Security Platform adds an extra layer of protection, making your smartphone experience worry-free. Take full advantage of these features to safeguard your digital world.

3. Connecting Seamlessly

Explore the world of high-speed connectivity with 5G and seamlessly connect to Wi-Fi, Bluetooth, and NFC. The Galaxy S24 Ultra is designed to keep you connected in every situation. Whether you're sharing your connection through mobile hotspot and tethering or embracing the era of 5G, the connectivity features of this device empower you to stay in touch with the world.

4. Mastering the Art of Photography

Elevate your photography skills with the revolutionary camera system of the Galaxy S24 Ultra. From capturing everyday moments to exploring advanced camera modes, this device is a true master in the art of photography. Discover the tips and tricks that make every shot a masterpiece and unravel the potential of your creative vision.

5. Personalising Your Experience

Make your Galaxy S24 Ultra an extension of yourself by delving into the world of themes and settings. Personalization is key, and the device offers a myriad of options to tailor it to your liking. From choosing themes to adjusting display settings, this chapter guides you on how to make your smartphone experience uniquely yours.

Staying Updated: Additional Resources

To ensure you stay ahead of the curve and make the most of your Galaxy S24 Ultra, it's essential to stay updated on additional resources. Samsung provides not only the user guide in various formats but also instructional videos and tutorials on their website and through the Samsung Members app. These resources can be valuable companions on your journey with the Galaxy S24 Ultra, offering visual insights and step-by-step guidance.

As you embark on your adventure with the Samsung Galaxy S24 Ultra, remember that this device is more than just a phone; it's a companion, a tool, and a gateway to a world of possibilities. Make the most of every feature, explore new horizons, and embrace the technological marvel that is the Galaxy S24 Ultra.

Here's to an unparalleled smartphone experience with your Samsung Galaxy S24 Ultra!

www.ingramcontent.com/pod-product-compliance
Lightning Source LLC
LaVergne TN
LVHW051716050326
832903LV00032B/4227